I0177088

Winds Upon Gentle Waves - Copyright 2019 © Enosh S. Lazarus
All rights reserved.

ISBN: 978-0-9996182-4-0 (Paperback)
ISBN: 978-0-9996182-5-7 (eBook)

Cover Design by III Designs
www.ismailben.com

Winds Upon Gentle Waves
Love, Loss & Life

Enosh S. Lazarus

LIFE

Soul

There was a soul, was born of pain
And shrieked she did, then cried of strain
But little she knew of her imminent bane
That she will have to cry again

She stepped ahead and bore a smile
It tried to stay and last a while
But drops of woe had wet her face
It swung at her, that fingered mace
Of all she asked, to be treated right
To have some love, to have a bite
But empty hearts and empty plates
The darkened nights, the endless fights
She slept away and ached within
Her heart was weak and body thin

Of all the close, a mother she called
Her heart was black, her love was walled
Her greed was lust, men came like flood
The least she knew her flesh and blood
She watched her breathe the death of cold
There was no father that she could hold
That hand she feared that galled her red
That aimed for her once the other was dead

She filled her eyes with wells of courage
To leave the prison and rise to flourish
Too bad for her, the prophecy unfolds
The world is harsh, as she was told
She gathered her spirit and marched on forward
She took it head on and faced all the horrors
The path was broken, she stumbled and fell
But went without fear, the streets of hell
With trails of sweat and streaks of tears
She marked her way throughout the years
To be where she's at, at the highest of all
To use those wings, but not to crawl
To fulfill the fate that was written at birth
To cry forever, but still have worth

(Continued)

Enosh S. Lazarus

That life had eased when love arrived
The feeling so new, she once deprived
They strolled together the gardens of bloom
And then she bore a seed in her womb
Afraid at first, she wept for a while
What life she'll give to her own child

She planted a rose, the purest of all
And cared for her, a beauty so small
She raised her well through sorrows that fell
But raised her strong to face the wrong
And when she blossomed, she scented of love
And gathered her close like wings of a dove
To watch her be a woman alike
In dark of world a flame alight

Her life was done, her purpose fulfilled
That once was lost, the trust rebuilt
And there she watched the splendor of her
The love, the daughter she wished she were
Upon a chair that rested at hearth
To see her name and seed on earth
So she may close her eyes in peace
And hope that dream may never cease

"Wisdom is like true love, not everybody finds it, not everybody accepts it, not everybody projects it, and not everybody protects it."

Enosh S. Lazarus

Prayer

I walked the aisle and wore the white
My creator at side in face alike
He held my hand and pressed it warm
Assured me days of love, few of storm

The hand that taught me stride
Was trembling still
The eyes that watched me smile
With tears were fill
At step upon step
His breaths were shrill
The distance shortened
And shook his will

When end approached, I turned to look
Released I was, but a moment he took
A phase of life that waited ahead
Prepared he was, but riddled with dread
That stranger had grasped my arm with yearn
Just claimed from him his lifetime's earn

He trudged afar and joined the pews
A man at loss, yet nothing to lose
A possession with which he was once blessed
A treasure reduced from a beautiful nest
Then came a smile, the most content
It now was mended, the will was bent
No more the time in sadness spent
She will be here, as far she went
He tapped his heart, uncaged it free
Then raised his hand for me to see
And I replied with tearful glee
That hand I'd held that made me me

And then he prayed and made a plea
For me the most and my man to be
To hold together when our skin would fold
Two hopelessly in love, two hopelessly old
May he love me then just as he loves me now
May it never be lost, the fidelity to a vow
When our bones are brittle and eyes are drain
When I wear the white on my head again

Enosh S. Lazarus

Winds Upon Gentle Waves

"The gusts of doubt are violent.
A trust in self is silent."

Enosh L. Lazarus

Dream

There she sat, sad in eyes, watched her own reflection fill
Pool of life, just ahead, rippled with imperfection still
The scars of loss, the bulk of curves, the flesh her own rejected ill
There she walks the weight of earth, no charm in her and beauty nil
She stood alone and glimpsed below, the plump of her beneath her skin
She wept at night and crept to sleep, the flesh, the size the skin to dream

There she was, the mist of dew, in her sight that blurred her view
Pool of life, glimmered tonight, her image she thought to find anew
The crease of scarce, the juts of bones, the lanky frame, in shame it grew
There she walks the gaunt, the lean, to look at her a pleasure to two
She stood alone and glimpsed below, the thin from which a breath she drew
She wept at night and crept to sleep, the flesh, the size the skin to dream

Across the pool of life they met, to blade their wrist was vice a debt
Relief they sought to all the woe, the pain, the curse, the tears aflow
Arose the two, beheld the dream, to mirror the rest, a pointless gleam
Rejoiced were they and sung of strength, the grace of soul, not size or length
A rose allures in splendor of whole, a petal apart shall turn to coal

Of all the women that ever lived, their deeds remembered or that they give
The heart that felt the pain of rest, that heart of love shall never divest
To those who deem a size to charm, do well to bring but self to harm
So live to breathe and free the chain, the scars, the dents, the flaws remain
From beauty of plus to glamour of thin, a rose they are from out and within

Enosh L. Lazarus

Winds Upon Gentle Waves

"Be harder than life and scarier than death, with a will to survive."

Enosh S. Lazarus

Wings

When skies defeat the hue of dark
And wings take flight toward the mark
When world shall lunge to drown me down
Then I shall rise to claim my crown

To bury the doubt and burn the taunt
To fight the villains, a life they've haunt
To all who delved holes in path
To push me in and mock my wrath
To watch me writhe in mire of lies
To put no end to weakened cries

I soared away, what wings have I
The heavens had bowed, I went so high
A sea of flames I swam across
Through scarce of gain and pain of loss

My wings were singed, that's all the harm
My spirit renewed and hopes to swarm
To stand where I would die today
For what my lovers live to prey
To sink the living corpse beneath
To tear with lips more than teeth
Rejoice they would to have their play
Until it dies and smokes away

But here I stand to take them on
To all the wounds and arrows drawn
The whip on me has lived so much
My soul this hurt will never touch
I breathe through all, invoke my fate
The hour is mine, the rest can wait

Enosh S. Lazarus

"Death isn't the only state that declares someone dead.
They could be living just like the rest of us and still be lifeless."

Enosh S. Lazarus

Heaven

The ground on which I breathed had looked
No different than the grave I've seized
This life I lived had gravely seemed
No different than the death I received

The love I had so much it suffered
No different than the pain I've owned
The cause that kept me breathing still
No different than my burial's shudder

The black of my grave would screech
In wait for worthless heart and flesh
Yet I smile in the arms of it
Awaiting another life past death

May it be not a children's dream
Fictitious myth we all believed
Unlike the lore of glee and love
I pray there lives a heaven above

But there it goes my life away
Abandoning all the tales of worth
There was no use of heart above
Then why we had a heart on earth

With wings they flew across the heavens
A specter of fire and sin below
The use of heart was befitting up here
On earth it had but hurt and woe

If laws of life were made to change
The high and low shall not collapse
For us to live on heaven and earth
If human were gifted a soul perhaps

Enosh S. Lazarus

Winds Upon Gentle Waves

"The best thing about dying is that you're finally remembered."

Enosh S. Lazarus

Battle

I watched a man who walked alone
Upon his back was a heavy load
Nothing he carried, but yet he was bent
I knew his life in poverty was spent

He strode on forward to a battle unseen
There stood no enemies, the way was clean
A wrinkle of worry on face he wore
And hands in burden of work were sore
His lips had trembled to whisper words alone
His gait was sunken and junctions would groan
He lost his strength about a mile back
There was no flesh, the skin met the bone
Yet he shuffled to a future unknown
A will to survive, a will of stone
The only certainty that stayed his mind
Days ahead be no different than those left behind

I saw his home that stood in ruins
The walls shall fall at the slightest doings
A scrawny little lad greeted doom before birth
To be born in a home that was destined to dearth
And there came another as hapless as the first
She limped against a crutch, a four year old curse
But opening into smiles, they explored with curiosity
Paths of life were few, yet they cared not for paucity
And there emerged a voice that called them up inside
There was the tree of strength that bore this fruit with pride
She made them sit close and served them all she had
She took it all from hers, her children's plates to add
To watch that smile that brightened her home and soul
That made her feel complete, made her feel whole

And when the veil of night came and the tired returned
The sound of laughter again and a fire that burned
That kept the house warm but the spirit warmer
This day was better still, better than the former
To know the future ahead will bear no miracle
To see their smiles makes life more livable
And all the day's troubles just buries into the dust
To know that love exists, in which we all trust

Enosh S. Lazarus

"The fruitless thing to give in today's world is your kindness to a stranger. You have no surety of it being returned."

Enosh S. Lazarus

Birth

The pearls that streaked the face of a child
Those eyes that filled when asked to smile
The fences and barbs of a war torn nation or
The ills of a greater front called home so wild

The tears that wept and the bodies that trembled
Their dreams were marked being orderly assembled
The innocence was lost, hearts emptied of hope
The dog watched guard, in bounds they'd lope
At the strike of fear they'd be put to sleep
But no one would see, if they'd rest or weep
The one who loved them and the one who bore
Their life they saw in chains across the metal door
A terror so great where the mind lost its senses
Little fingers entwined with chain linked fences

But there it happened, the calamity of old
Where walls would shatter and chains would fold
A deluge of love that flooded to the core
To heed our humanity, not an angry roar
And children would dash to their guardians again
To laugh till dawn and release the pain
To know their life was never a burden
And know their birth was not in vain

Enosh S. Lazarus

"I prayed for peace while they preyed for a piece."

Enosh S. Lazarus

Paths

I saw it when dusk dwindled
I saw it when dawn arose
I saw it when they fell asleep
I saw it when the world awoke
A dreary cloud in the sky alone
That's spent in time which once had flown
To cover the distance, one flight at a time
A milestone came, but far from home

I saw it in the dark, I saw it in the light
To walk through betrayal, to walk through fright
Ceaseless flares, the fires would burn
Fearless yet my eyes were stern
Bow to none, cry to none
Let no one beat you down to none

Twist away the face of fate
That stares you down the eyes to dare
Twist away the path of fear
That chars your soul within to scare
The trinity of life and then to the doom
There is no breath to draw in tomb
So break the chains of arrant gloom
And rise above the rest and loom

You're the one, you're it
All else shall follow the path you lit
Let all drop down low and wonder
Why did we wrong this mighty thunder?

Enosh S. Lazarus

Winds Upon Gentle Waves

"My life has been a fair of faces
Some fared well, others farewelled."

Enosh S. Lazarus

Stranger

The dreams of a sleepless night
How blurred they were
The colors of dark
That I couldn't tell
The dawn came across
And shattered them again
How sweet they were
The tales of the dead

The light of reality
To forget that haunts
The poor heart breathes
Remembering it all
The prison of pain
To escape it now
The time's right
The end of a fall

For once I follow
The path of my fate
To stand at the edge
Of love and hate
The world is a stranger
I know no one
In just one step
And I'll be done

Enosh S. Lazarus

"From the bouquets of a birth to the festoons of the graveyard, the cost of human adoration is the ruin of nature's gardens."

Enosh S. Lazarus

Childhood

The age of innocent childhood
O' where have I lost you
Come back to me wherever you've gone
I can't grow old without you

To jump across the logs of wood
To mind no more the rebukes of old
To run across the train tracks
To escape those household scold

The stars throughout a silent night
From one to other my fingers leap
To count them all I just might
Before I drift off to sleep

Those rides were fast against the wind
One after another the wheels would spin
Against the woods that stood a century
The eight year olds would easily win

The tales in bed came after all
The will to embark on adventure would call
And when the curtains of stories were flipped
I traveled the worlds within those walls

I wasn't alone, there were more than one
But where they strayed, I've spoken to none
Vanished from life, yet lost in living
We've fought many battles, but haven't won

To join our hands and search for the past
Let's come together in the end at last
In life to make a final endeavor
May we live just once before lost forever

Enosh S. Lazarus

"The saddest human death is the sight of a grave before him
and a life behind that was never lived."

Enosh S. Lazarus

Sorrows

I write of sorrows, I write of pain
I write of suffering, that'd never wane
I bear no fame, forgot my name
The world's a stage, my part never came

Tattered pages of my life, a long forgotten book
Scatter in the windy nights, no one cares to look
I kept them safe until I lived, but when its guard I could not stay
When the night had come to take, they became a child's play

Through aches of sorrow, I lived through stings of pain
I wept at misery and failures, I suffered my bane
Oh how the way I prayed, to face the big and small
I walked with my head high, to take the deepest fall
So in the late before I sleep, I may say I did it all
How much in this dark alone, I wish I didn't make that call

They flip the last of the page, the high winds that blow
It came to its tragic end, the book of my woe
Perhaps the window was left open, perhaps the door wasn't shut
And as the fluttering curtains would fall, my part in play was cut
So with nothing left to deliver or nothing more to achieve
I take an exit now, this world of performances I leave

Enosh S. Lazarus

Winds Upon Gentle Waves

"Time without Life is as frightening as Life without Time."

Enosh S. Lazarus

Promises

They loathed me back, all those I loved
And that I believed, did broke my trust
Delivered to an end, by all that I had
And all that I wished, abandoned me to dust

Six feet under, I rested for eternity
I read myself in dark and checked for absurdity
Mistakes that were made, evils were committed
Too large some crimes, to never be acquitted

I pray to rise again, to correct all the wrong
I promise to be good, I promise to be strong
But remove all the rest, I need no strangers along
I breathed my first alone, won't die amidst a throng

A life that once I had, the one I never knew
Just let me have it again, to see it finally through

Enosh S. Lazarus

Winds Upon Gentle Waves

"We've gathered to lighten our hearts.
Let's talk about the liberty of death and not bonds of living."

Enosh S. Lazarus

Fears

I looked out the window and watched for a while
The time was past midnight, a drizzle made me smile
A draft of breeze was upon my face
My skin a thousand droplets traced

And then I saw what shared my life
All out afar in lonesome nights
It breathed in peace, yet quivered in quiet
It yearned for much at unmeasured heights

The fears had gone just past the hour
The life was short but why so sour
To stand alone and vulnerable there
Aloof amidst a people's fair
Yet there sparked the silver gleams
It bloomed at the tide of dreams
The beauty and its strength so pure
To stand that many nights obscure

When comes the hour of glory and luster
The beauties of the world in spirit shall fluster
Not one does eye the splendor we share
Our time will come, to gods I swear
And they shall all in wonder stare
One here on earth, the other up there

Enosh S. Lazarus

"People have mistaken flattery for friendship these days."

Enosh S. Lazarus

Lost

O let me be lost without you
For once I wish to die
So that I may find myself too
And pride in it I tried

The pain to all you give
Have no more of a prize
From young to old, you pity none
You're cruel to dumb and wise

To have you is a curse
To bear you a burden
You come to us as a gift
That hides in nothing but lies

The dreams you brought along
At night that stole my sleep
The heart you vowed to find
The one shall love me deep
A flight to the highest of all
The crown I toiled to seek
Where are the times you pledged
The dawn of hope I've ached to breathe

O let me be lost without you
For once I wish to live
It may be arrant dark in there
But it has my peace to give

Enosh S. Lazarus

<u>LOSS</u>

Enosh S. Lazarus

Winds Upon Gentle Waves

"The one who's had a shattered heart,
knows the value of broken glass."

Enosh S. Lazarus

Tombstone

It was the saddest expression of love ever uttered
Upon a cold concrete tombstone
And the edge of it was dabbed
With the perfect pearls of sorrow
I love you, she said
To a soul that never left

Enosh S. Lazarus

Winds Upon Gentle Waves

"The season of heartbreaks is over
Can we be strangers again?"

Enosh S. Lazarus

Parted

The lips that spoke the lies of love
They need me not, the broken word
Then why they filled, the eyes above
The truth was which, I saw or heard

Your words were soft when lights awoke
Your touch was warm when darkness broke
Your thoughts were pure when dusk embarked
Your sight of me and all it sparked

The songs we sung by the showering shore
The sound of waves, the music we adore
No poets we were, the words a bit mindless
We had our laughs, a feeling that is timeless

The summer still ripples, the ocean we splashed
The winter still cracks, the snow we dashed
But parted have we, our ways of heart
Yet summer awaits and winter departs

Enosh S. Lazarus

"A touch of indifference made all the difference."

Enosh S. Lazarus

Bowed

You leashed to your feet, a woman afraid
I took it as a gift, I bowed and obeyed
I served your want for flesh you hungered
At times I felt my breaths were numbered

You pushed me back, I crawled to you
You made me kneel, I worshipped you
You gave me away, I longed for you
You did it all, I still absolved you

But when your scourge I could take no more
And when the thought of escape arrived
The day I rose, to me I swore
I'll take from you the things deprived
Your life dispatched, my freedom revived
I pierced your heart, black filth on floor
And that's the tale how I survived

Enosh S. Lazarus

Winds Upon Gentle Waves

A lot needs to be said
A lot needs to be done
But needs came in the way
A lot of them

Enosh S. Lazarus

Winds Upon Gentle Waves

"Was it the fault of time or the foible of our tempers
that once in love, we never loved?"

Enosh S. Lazarus

Apart

Of all the time we spent apart
The price of which a stream of tears
Now once together our shattered hearts
Throughout the count of imminent years

For me to weep for old time's sake
To drain the pools of quaking pain
I bow my head and freely take
The fond embrace of your arms again

Enosh S. Lazarus

"I never realized life without you would be worthless
until I became worthy of you."

Enosh S. Lazarus

Strangers

At least we would've fantasized about us
Or could have despised each other
At least we'd have some expectations
If we were rather strangers than lovers

At least we would have stories to share
And have miles to discover
At least we would have a lot to say
If we were rather strangers than lovers

At least we would've smiled when crossing paths
Or would have dreamt in dark covers
At least we would have believed in love
If we were rather strangers than lovers

At least we would've wished us well
Or suffer heartbreak but recover
At least we wouldn't hate each other
If we were rather strangers than lovers

Enosh S. Lazarus

Winds Upon Gentle Waves

"The greatest exchange I've made
had to be a heart full of love for a heart full of ache."

Enosh I. Lazarus

Hurt

The days of love gave signs of bliss
I found a perfect man
But then emerged the man who hid
Your words misplaced, your acts amiss

I warned you not to make me weep
A wonder of life you are
A knife I put to your deceit
I'd bury it real deep

A man of dreams, a man of will
I am a destroyer of worlds
No lies in it, but truth be told
A hand stained in blood's a thrill

You kneel before, I jump and shrill
Put a sparkling seal on me
But reach the altar in time or else
I'd burn you alive and bury you still

Your children without pain I bear
But love us till you breathe
You bring about any hurt to us
Your organs shall I tear

Let me grow now old with you
Let's die hand in hand
If you ever refuse I'd still grow old
But not the way I've planned

Enosh S. Lazarus

Winds Upon Gentle Waves

"I would've survived the marketplace if I knew love was a trade."

Enosh S. Lazarus

Grief

The more you strain to shatter it now
The more it yearns for you
My callow heart and its thousand bits
It still won't come to rue

The day you chose to walk past
Without a sight of me
It wasn't just my eyes that cried
My heart had wept for me

Now yours shall weep a thousand tears
For all you've done today
And all you'll miss throughout your life
Because you stayed away

A want to see not a ray of light
When two of us come together
But time has brought the world between
And distanced us forever

Now fallen from sight, can't share the light
But I've loved you even then
Ocean without water, body without breath
I've felt so time and again

How hard it is to hide a grief
Behind a veil of tears
How hard it is to bear the pain
Beyond the wound of fears

Yet still recall the days of bliss
How splendor is at its high
To be called into love without a voice
Like a heartbeat and twinkle of the eye

Enosh S. Lazarus

Winds Upon Gentle Waves

"The value of a dream is that drop of tear in which it's spent."

Enosh S. Lazarus

Mistakes

If it ever brought death to a man
Let me witness mine tonight
As I see you in love with him
My true happiness in sight

Fate led us both to a stone of a heart
Or were those our mistakes that gifted us a part
For one half to you, I'll share the other
Incomplete as can be, now and forever

You tried to join it at times, to pair it with others
But stones are cut deep, like shattered lovers
You hold it still in hand and plead them all to be
The match is just with one, it joins like lock to a key

Enosh S. Lazarus

"The world in which we live, a heart's worth is lesser than a pint of liquor, a dance move and some laughs."

Enosh S. Lazarus

Wept

The season of blossoms came and went
Those that welted stayed and wept
We might have found a garden of bloom
But winter came and left its gloom
Those arid remains of a purest want
The storms had swept, left wither to haunt
Wish I had cried the tears you shed
Wish you had smiled in my stead
Never hoped for a garden
A wilderness would have survived
Never hoped for land at large
A corner of it would have sufficed

Enosh S. Lazarus

Corpse

Do you hear the sounds, the cry of plea
The smoke that comes from the ruins of me
It begs to live that corpse of mine
Your love has finally set me free

Drink to my death tonight
The red on my head tonight
If you are left hungry still
Feed on my flesh tonight
It is without a breath tonight
Take the spoils of my worship
To make a feast of infidelity
May you find it in that god of gold
That you chose over love tonight

Enosh S. Lazarus

"He spoke the truth and couldn't even lie.
It was a sorrow that could only be hidden with a smile."

Enosh S. Lazarus

Winds Upon Gentle Waves

In a pool of life I dove headfirst
To quench my soul with a drop of love
An age went by and I watched accursed
The pool would brim, but I drowned of thirst

Enosh S. Lazarus

"Heartbreak is the only calamity that doesn't make a sound."

Enosh S. Lazarus

Yours

If I ever spoke, the name was yours
If I ever dreamt, the face was yours
If I ever yearned, the touch was yours
If I ever longed, the love was yours
When I arose to the riches
When I fell to the ditches
If I ever despaired, the absence was yours
If I ever gained, the audience was yours
And my love for you arose to such extremes
That if I ever breathed, the breath was yours
That if I ever died, the death was… never yours

Enosh S. Lazarus

"To lose yourself in an endless stream of recovery
is better than holding onto its remains."

Enosh S. Lazarus

Tears

There was afar a gathering above
Where I too went in search for love
Hoping to find a broken heart there
To mend my own with kindred care

I saw the men and women of sorts
And all rejoiced but love was short
They were of want and lust and need
They called it love, it wasn't indeed

I saw her there, a stranger apart
I patched my wounds of an aching heart
She danced and sang in arm with him
But bore a sorrow, a lack within

True love was what she left me for
If tears are it, I want no more

Enosh S. Lazarus

Winds Upon Gentle Waves

"The tale is uniquely short, I died before I died."

Enosh S. Lazarus

<u>LOVE</u>

Enosh S. Lazarus

Winds Upon Gentle Waves

"Love's a tale of two hearts that breathed existence into it."

Enosh S. Lazarus

Slave

The seasons that we lived apart
The years that simply darted past
The days and nights we ached alone
And longed for them to never last

I never knew I could fall so much
To rise in your love to an extent
Where I'd breathe at your command
And die at your heart's content

The time is lost when I owned myself
I've forsaken my soul to you
What was my gain out of this surrender
That I am your slave anew

Enosh S. Lazarus

"Call me pretty again, and I'll haunt you until the day you die."

Enosh S. Lazarus

Drown

I never wept for a dream
To have it come to an end
If endless had they ever been
If only you were in them

I never wanted to wake
To watch the morning sun unfold
Until the nights I suffered for
Your warm embrace in dark and cold

A heart that beat along the age
Had never stopped in time
You stole away a couple of beats
Like a burglar commits a crime

Had never ached to be so lost
And felt but stolen ever
Until you took away all I had
Robbing me from myself forever

What is life without you next to me
Like a heart without a breath
Like peace derived when all that ends
Like a soul delivered to death

Like sun and stars that sink in time
I drown in love with you
Let's share a similar glimmer of light
To live when life is through

Enosh S. Lazarus

Winds Upon Gentle Waves

"How beautiful it is for two strangers to realize
they would grow old together."

Enosh S. Lazarus

Surrender

A love that wilted across the desert
To bloom for a change in tender care
A place that is warm and full of seasons
Your heart is an answer to that one prayer

I take that pride to kneel before you
Like a drop of dew that lives to adorn
And when that beauty it has enriched
It slips into death past every morn

Observe the red droplets of dew
I surrender to you a bleeding heart
To keep it or forsake, I leave to you
Either take it whole, or tear it apart

Enosh S. Lazarus

"I'd be madly, crazily in love if you ever broke my heart."

Enosh S. Lazarus

Light

Let the night remain with its inky sky
And the light of black may never die
Let no moon to drown in sad embrace
Let no dusk rise to take its place
Let us sit at shores and love forever
Let the dark remain and leave us never
For me to sit and gaze you away
As dusk departs and dawns you gray
A touch of simple moonlit glare
To burn your face with beauty flare
It all reflects where a glimmer lies
Is that an ocean or just your eyes?

Enosh S. Lazarus

"Falling in love with you, still falling,
it's been a while haven't reached the bottom yet."

Enosh S. Lazarus

You

Of all the mountains and seas around us
The sight I wish to see
Is You

Of all the places of the world
That one I wish to belong
Is You

Of all the relationships that ever existed
The one I wish to have
Is You

Of all the pride amongst us
To whom I'd raise my head
Is You

Of all the hurt and pain in the world
The one I wish to receive
Is You

Of all the lovers in the dreams
That one I dreamt to have
Is You

Of all the abundance of life on this planet
This life I wish to live
Is You

That no more may know this truth
This secret I wish to share
Is You

Enosh S. Lazarus

"You had belonged to me since the beginning.
I just found you yesterday."

Enosh S. Lazarus

She

By the shores of the sea, she still thinks of me
With her eyes half closed, the old memories imposed
A subdued laughter at the edge of sunsets
The traces of simple thoughts and regrets

Had she just called my name through a soft whisper
Had she just draped herself against the frigid winter
A smile had followed on her face that reeked of longing
She couldn't let go of me, like a treasured belonging

There she murmured my name again
Breathed me into her heart's domain
Remembered the sound of my voice once more
Shivered at my touch and felt to the core
Just as twilight came and blew a gentle cold
She yearned for my embrace and a warm, tender hold

Enosh S. Lazarus

Winds Upon Gentle Waves

"Are there any more extremes of love than to be
woken up by worldly dreams from the reality of you?"

Enosh S. Lazarus

Sleepless

Brimming with a sparkle of youth
Shone with a glimmer of life
Like mirrors of the vast ocean
That rippled in a sleepless strife

Until I saw them, I was simply restless
And now we've met, my want is endless
To drown in them so fearlessly
To read them through for eternity

I tried some words, to try to tell
They weren't expressive enough to describe them well
I attempted to paint a beauty so divine
No colors were vivid to make them alive

They breathed like a winter cold mist
They beat like a heart is sunshine kissed
They pierced a soul and filled in thought
To all the life the peace they brought
They pitied the poor, and corrected the wicked
They loved the innocent, and eased the livid

What more could I sing, in praise of them
The magical two like stars of gem
At times in laughter the way they winked
And first we met they slightly blinked

Enosh S. Lazarus

Winds Upon Gentle Waves

"They say that you never die once you're in love.
My dilemma is how to stay alive until I do."

Enosh S. Lazarus

Alive

Is it a trick of the mind or play of silly thoughts
Or have you really smiled at me and shared my sight
The decades of my life were like ruins of an age
That one gaze of glee made it a beautiful paradise
Like a dream finds its place in the dreams of a dreamer
Like a sail finds it worth in the winds upon gentle waves
To that wail of life that cringed with horror and pain
You've entered it as a new breath that makes one alive again

Enosh S. Lazarus

"What's more beautiful than a gilded veil of daylight upon her face and a glimmer of love in her eyes?"

Enosh S. Lazarus

Questions

I had some questions if you don't mind
Answer them honestly if you'd be kind
Why do I feel alone when in a crowd?
Why does my heart flail when you are around?
Why does the world seem a better place to live?
Why do I simply surrender all I have to give?
Why the sights of the world seem beautiful with you?
Why the days fly by but the nights can't get through?
The mountains, the rivers, the wonders of the world?
Yet the greatest wonder is the view when your lips would curl
Why am I senseless, speechless, and heartless all of a sudden?
When your eyes meet mine and I'm all but sullen?
Neither you seem to say anything, nor I the capacity to tell
It's been almost an age, well, quite a while in love I fell
Tell me now if this were a myth, to believe in life after death?
What is love if this isn't it, to take your name at final breath?

Enosh S. Lazarus

Winds Upon Gentle Waves

"The day I learn to count my flaws as perfection,
I'd love myself just as much as you do."

Enosh S. Lazarus

Whispers

Let me confess to you in simple whispers
A whisper cooler than the breeze at night
A whisper softer than your touch at times
A whisper lighter than a flake that wafts
A whisper that travels the silent drafts
A whisper that escapes the great crowds
A whisper that watches the dreams in shrouds
A whisper that's damp as the morning mist
A whisper that's moist as your lips after kiss
A whisper that reeks after an age of rain
A whisper that shines like moonlit plains
A whisper like your wet body after bath
A whisper at night on the firefly path
A whisper that outlasts the day and through
And reaches your ears to say, I love you

Enosh S. Lazarus

"There it came, there it went.
The moment we'd met, the lifetime we'd spent."

Enosh S. Lazarus

Euphoria

Is it your love for me or simply my want of you
They way to you treat me ill, yet can't do without you
I'm resolved to be yours whether you have me or not
Whip me, bash me, throw me, have me buried or shot

If you ever wish to test my love, just leave me for a while
If you return and find me alive, illusions of eyes are vile
The worst euphoria there can be is being drunk with love
Like a glass emptied before you, when you haven't sipped a drop

I wish it stayed as it was given to me
To let me have a share of a price I paid
The tricks and trials I failed bit by bit

And just as it vanished, I felt again
A hand across my throat
Never moist, it was hot and dry
And my neck it easily scorched

I lost all breath there was none left
Until the glass filled again
But served across the table tonight
A helpless loss, a wantless gain

Enosh S. Lazarus

"I hope you wouldn't mind if
I lived at the mercy of your love."

Enosh S. Lazarus

Suffer

One sight, one soul
One want, one goal
To never part
A soft whisper
Let me suffer in love
Helpless, heartless
In thorns and blooms
The garden that looms
Lost I long to be
A storm that comes
The cloud that grays
The wind that sways
The word that preys
Lost in love
Lost in dreams
Let's sleep forever
The arms of a beloved
My eternal rest

Enosh S. Lazarus

Winds Upon Gentle Waves

"What is love if there are no heartaches and partings?
The will to reunite makes it immortal."

Enosh S. Lazarus

Winds Upon Gentle Waves

Song

The troubles of the day
Let's put them away
Pray the night stay
And the dawn delay
Let me give you rest
And all you need
Let me hum you a song
And put you to sleep

Enosh S. Lazarus

Winds Upon Gentle Waves

"The scent of the perfume I wore the night before
arose from more than your skin, your soul."

Enosh S. Lazarus

Novels by Enosh S. Lazarus

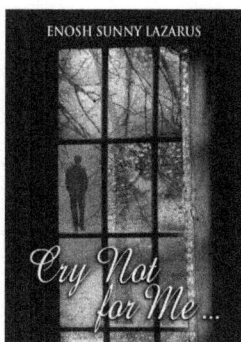

www.ingramcontent.com/pod-product-compliance
Lightning Source LLC
Chambersburg PA
CBHW031548040426
42452CB00006B/235